Praise for S

"Refreshing, inspiring, and though...
paced stories weave historical facts with character education and a
sprinkle of 'can do spirit.' With the historical context and questions to
prompt higher level thinking, there is no additional prep needed! *Six
Revolutionary WOW Factor Women* is a must-have for all traditional and
homeschool classrooms."

—Jenny Leeds, K-6 teacher, gifted specialist

"These are beautifully crafted but seldom-told stories of brave and
resourceful colonial American women who changed history—women
who are role models to inspire today's girls to do the same."

—Clare Britcher, retired York County, Virginia, Master Gardener, York
County School Division Volunteer of the Month 2006, and mother of a
daughter in STEM

"Having been an actor and tour guide in southeastern Virginia for
the last fifty years, I have met many storytellers of note. Without a doubt,
Heidi Hartwiger is among the very best. She weaves her story magic
with the mastery of a craftsman, not only entertaining but enlightening
her audience so they learn while thoroughly enjoying themselves. It is a
gift sorely needed in a time when knowledge and history must compete
with the constant distractions of our modern world."

—Woody Chapman, actor, director, playwright, and tour guide in the
Williamsburg, Virginia, area

"Heidi Hartwiger brings historical figures to life in a very engaging
book. This fascinating collection of stories, featuring inspiring women
of the colonial period, is perfect for integrating character education into
history lessons. It spotlights positive character traits and encourages
young readers to discover the same in themselves. This is enjoyable
reading for the student of history and a valuable resource for parents
and educators."

—Linda Buck, retired teacher, Newport News, Virginia, public schools

"My friend Heidi's deep knowledge of colonial American history
and unique gift of storytelling come together in this collection of stories.
Each of the six vignettes is not only interesting and educational; each
sparks the imagination and challenges its readers to find their own way
to say WOW— 'Watch Out World!'"

—Pastor Donald Stuppy

"I enjoyed reading *Six Revolutionary WOW Factor Women*. I can envision young girls, and even boys like my eleven-year-old grandson, learning to recognize and use their own WOW Factor to help their community. The examples of the profiled girls and women, all from different walks of life, be they enslaved, Native American, or colonist, points to the contributions we can all make, no matter our age or personal background."

—Kay Larrieu, retired educator

"WOW, indeed. It's hard to imagine so much motivation and socially relevant historical information could be packed into such a small book. Like the characters included in these pages, Hartwiger clearly shouts, 'Watch Out World! I can deal with this.' Inspirational, enriching, and empowering, this is a must read for future leaders. Read it early and read it often. The spirit of American Women is alive in these pages."

—Don Feenerty, community development executive

"Weaving her words into fascinating stories, Heidi Hartwiger introduces us to one woman after another, each of whom made an incredible contribution to our country, to democracy, to freedom. From a schoolteacher of enslaved children to an Oneida Indian maiden to a President's wife, she takes us through the records of history to describe feats of courage and cunning that helped to save not only children and families but also soldiers and artifacts. The six incredible women she describes represent several of the thirteen original American colonies and offer models to be revered in today's society. Her thought-provoking questions about each heroine give readers opportunity to continue pondering the stories she so skillfully recounts."

—Grace Toney Edwards, Ph.D., Professor Emerita of Appalachian Studies and English, Radford University, Radford, Virginia

HEIDI HARTWIGER

SIX

REVOLUTIONARY

FACTOR
WOMEN

Brandylane
Publishers, Inc.

ISBN: 978-1-958754-39-9
Library of Congress Control Number: 2023902609

Illustrations by Emily Hurst Pritchett

Designed by Sami Langston
Production management by Haley Simpkiss

Printed in the United States of America

Published by
Brandylane Publishers, Inc.
5 S. 1st Street
Richmond, Virginia 23219

Brandylane
Publishers, Inc.
Publishing books since 1985

brandylanepublishers.com

To Margaret . . . the girl who loved history.

Contents

Introduction

These are the stories of six strong, determined, and independent women who lived in colonial America's thirteen colonies around the time of the Revolutionary War. As you read, you will discover how each found her WOW factor.

So, what exactly is the WOW factor? It's a special quality tucked down deep inside you, which comes out when a problem needs solving. It might come from love, courage, or perseverance. Whatever inspires it, it is the part of you that says, "Watch Out World! I can deal with this."

In these pages, you'll meet women like Ann Wager, who taught in the first school for children of the enslaved. Or Elizabeth Freeman, who was the first enslaved person to be legally declared free by a high court in Massachusetts. Polly Cooper was an Oneida Indian woman who walked four hundred miles with corn to feed Washington's starving troops at Valley Forge.

Nancy Morgan Hart outsmarted the Redcoats on the home front. The Cherokee called her "War Woman." At age sixteen, Betty Zane ran through enemy lines with an apron full of black gunpowder to save Fort Henry. Dolley Madison, James Madison's wife, made curious ice cream from French recipes as First Lady. When the British invaded Washington, DC, legend has it that Dolley removed a portrait of George Washington before she fled the White House so the British would not "capture George."

Maybe as you read these stories, you will discover your own WOW factor!

Ann Wager
1716-1774

In the year 1716, Williamsburg, Virginia, was a prosperous town under British rule. By the late 1760s, many people began to worry and grumble about strict British laws. Rumors of higher taxes swirled.

Nevertheless, people continued their daily routines. They went to church on Sunday, and early every morning they shopped in the Market Square for fresh eggs, meat, fruits, and vegetables. On occasional Saturdays, a Fair Day was held in the Market Square, and all the town's children—both of free families and those who were indentured or enslaved—had a chance to enjoy foot races, jugglers, and musicians.

Many rich, educated men became ministers or lawyers. Wealthy and middle-class women organized their households, embroidered beautiful linens, and served elegant meals.

But if a woman was widowed—especially a woman who was not wealthy—her world turned upside down. With no money of her own, how could she support her children? A widow might take over her husband's business or use her skills in sewing to become a seamstress. And if she was lucky enough to have a formal education, she could teach.

Suppose you lived in those days and something terrible happened, and you were the only one who could support your family. What would you do? Assuming you could read and write, would you choose to earn lots of money teaching the children of wealthy Williamsburg families? Or would you rather make a little bit of money teaching children of enslaved parents who worked in local shops, taverns, and the homes of the wealthy families? In this story, set in the town of Williamsburg in the Eighteenth Century, just before the Revolutionary War, you will discover the choice Ann Wager made.

A MOST UNUSUAL SCHOOL

She could embroider beautiful shawls, she could serve delicious meals, and she could read. At this time, it was usually only boys who could read, write, and cipher. But Ann Wager's father had made sure she was as well-educated as any boy. For many years, she was happily married, raising her son, William, and her young daughter, Mary. Then tragedy struck when Ann's husband died. William was nearly grown and ready to leave home, and Ann's husband had left her a bit of money. But she still needed a way to support herself and Mary. With her good education, she became a teacher. Sometimes Ann taught the children of wealthy families in their homes, while some students came to her home for lessons.

Several years passed. One particular afternoon, after her students had gone home, Ann started scrubbing and chopping potatoes and carrots for a stew, relieved that the school day was over. As she worked, she thought about a problem she was having with some of the little boys she taught. *I need a better way to teach Psalm 23. I can't get beyond saying, "The Lord is my shepherd" without the boys leaping and baa-baaing like sheep. This behavior is getting on my nerves.*

Shadows of night began creeping across the road. As Ann lit some candles, her heart flip-flopped a bit. Mary, now a grownup, had not returned from her daily errands. *Where is that girl?* Ann wondered. She listened for the familiar clip-clop of horses' hooves on the cobblestone street.

At last, through the open window, Ann heard Mary's voice rising above the clatter of approaching carriage wheels.

"Mother! Mother!" Mary shouted as the carriage came to a stop.

Wiping her hands on her apron, Ann hustled to open the door. It was unlike Mary to be so loud. Mary didn't even wait for the carriage driver to lower the steps for her. Leaving several parcels in the carriage, she lifted her blue woolen skirt above her shoes and jumped to the cobblestones. With her brown eyes as round as saucers, she grabbed her mother's hands. "I stopped by William Hunter's print shop to pick up your order, and something unbelievable happened!"

"Whatever it was must have been more exciting than watching Mr. Hunter set type for the next issue of the *Virginia Gazette*," said Ann.

"He had a visitor from Philadelphia. Guess who?" Mary's eyes danced. "Here's a clue: Who was so curious about electricity that he tied a key to a kite and flew it during a thunderstorm?"

Ann gasped. "Benjamin Franklin? Benjamin Franklin is here in Williamsburg?"

"Indeed! From what I saw, Mr. Franklin and Mr. Hunter are really good friends."

Ann thought for a moment. "That makes sense. They work in the printing business and both are post-masters."

Mary smiled. "I'll bet Mr. Hunter quotes from Mr. Franklin's *Poor Richard's Almanac* in the *Virginia Gazette*."

Ann chuckled. "Do you remember Mr. Franklin's words that I tell my little scholars every day?"

"'Tis easier to prevent bad habits than to break them.'" Mary knew this quote by heart. "My manners were not the best. I confess I listened to their conversation. I think Mr. Franklin was asked by people in England to find a location for a school . . . a school for children of the enslaved."

As it turned out, a major reason Benjamin Franklin had visited Williamsburg was indeed to locate a place for a school to educate children of the enslaved and indentured servants. At this time, in many of the thirteen colonies, enslaved people and indentured servants were forbidden to read and write. But in Virginia, this was not so.

Williamsburg had been picked as the perfect place for the school. At the nearby College of William and

Mary, young men studied to become ministers. So, in 1760, a school called the Bray School—funded by an English clergyman, the Reverend Thomas Bray, and his associates—opened under the care of the College of William and Mary. The directors of the school wanted the very best teacher. Since both boys and girls would come to the Bray School, the directors decided a woman would be perfect for the role. Their number-one choice? Ann Wager!

The little house where the classes would be taught was near the college. Ann moved into the school, and Mary stayed at the family home to take care of it.

Before the school opened, Ann had many visits with Reverend Thomas Dawson, the president of the College of William and Mary. He was her supervisor.

"Mrs. Wager, as you see, we have arranged wooden benches for student seating," he said, pointing to one area of the main room. "When the benches are full, the younger students may be seated on the floor."

"How many students will attend?" Ann asked.

"You could have anywhere from twenty to thirty boys and girls who live in town. They will arrive early in the morning and will walk back to their homes before dark."

"And their ages?"

"As young as three and as old as eight," the reverend said. "The plan is for them to attend a three-year term. I want dedicated students. I don't want the children coming and going willy-nilly." Reverend Dawson was a no-nonsense person. "The Bray School is for education, not childcare. As part of their Christian education, your students will learn to read and recite scripture. Every Sunday, you will escort your students to church."

To Ann's thinking, Reverend Dawson seemed rather stern. She knew teaching would be a challenge, but it was a challenge she happily accepted. She could never have taught so many children at once in her home. So, in the days leading up to the school's opening, she was excited to be organizing a classroom and planning lessons.

Ann's classroom was full of bright sunlight that streamed in through the windows. Along one wall was a big brick fireplace to warm them on winter days. *I love this room*, she thought, smiling as she dusted the shelves along another wall. *I will put the slates and slate pencils for writing on the lowest shelf. The books for religious training will fit on the middle shelf, along with whatever food the children might bring.* Ann sighed and moved her hands along the rough wooden benches. *I wish there were desks for the older children*, she thought. But she knew she'd make do, just as she always had.

Ann chose to keep the sewing basket, filled with fabrics, colored yarns, and needles, on the top shelf. She knew children were curious, and embroidery needles could be a dangerous temptation. She looked all around the room. Something was missing. *Apples!* she thought. *That's it! I'll keep a basket of crunchy red apples in the corner. I'm not required to feed my students, but I know children. Hungry children can't learn, and they won't behave.*

School activities were planned according to the guidelines given to Ann by Reverend Dawson and the Bray School sponsors. The boys were to learn reading, writing, and math—called "ciphering" at the time— along with catechism and scripture. The girls' path was similar, except that embroidery would take the place of ciphering. Ann paused for a moment to think. *Yes,* she decided, *although it hasn't been asked of me, I will gladly add the challenge of teaching social skills. These children will be more successful in life if they have good manners. I certainly don't need books for that.*

The sunshine's fading fingers trailed along the well-swept floor, then up and over the shelves lining the walls as if to check Ann's teaching supplies were all in order before night fell. All was ready. The next day, the room would hum with children's voices and maybe even laughter. *How shall I settle the students and get each day off to a good start?* As Ann wrapped her shawl around her shoulders, she noticed the playful lambs embroidered around the edges. *Bible stories,* she thought. *That's it! I will tell them the story of how God told Noah to build an ark, and then we can read it in scripture.* She smiled. *I will make it clear before we begin that the classroom is not Noah's Ark. Animal sounds and leaping and bounding are fine, so long as they save it for outdoors.*

Still, she worried. Would her new students listen to her? Or, when they heard the story of Noah and the

Ark, would thirty voices bark, meow, cluck, and moo? Would they whinny like horses or make little lamb sounds like the children she'd tutored in the past?

Knock–Knock–Knock.

The sound jolted Ann from her daydreaming. She opened the door. It was Reverend Dawson. "I've brought the list of children who will be attending school tomorrow. Your students have parents who serve some of the best families, including the Peyton Randolph and Robert Carter Nicholas households. I understand Christiana Campbell will send children from her tavern as well. No doubt Jane Vope will want the children at the King's Arms Tavern out from underfoot."

Ann checked the list. "Perhaps I'll recognize some children. They may be in the group I see playing along Duke of Gloucester Street. I always fear that one day they will fall under carriage wheels or be trampled by horses."

"I wish you well, Mrs. Wager," Reverend Dawson said as he stepped out into the cool evening air. "Don't worry about firewood. I will see that someone from the college delivers and stacks it for you. You will always have a good supply."

In the blink of an eye, it was the first day of school. Ann was awake at sunrise. Her breakfast was biscuits and boiled eggs. For an extra good start, she drank two cups of hot tea with honey, then headed into her classroom to prepare for the day. School was about to begin. Thoughts were a jumble in her head. Would the children be happy or anxious or wild? Wrapping her lamb-embroidered shawl tightly around her shoulders, she read and reread the list of more than two dozen names. Matching so many names and faces at once would be a challenge.

Before she could see them, Ann heard children's voices coming closer and closer. Smiling, she stood by the open door with a special greeting for each child. "Good morning and welcome," she said, extending her hand for every student to shake as they entered. "I am Mrs. Wager, and your name is?"

Some children were too shy to speak or even sit down. Once they had all filed in, Ann looked at her students, then looked at the empty wooden benches. *No, I won't have them sit on those uncomfortable, backless benches,* she decided.

"All right, everybody, find a place on the floor to sit," she said. The students sat, younger children snuggled up to the older ones. From then on, each morning, the children sat together on the floor to begin the day. What do you suppose the boys and girls heard on their very first morning at the Bray School and every morning that followed?

After telling her class the story of Noah and the Ark, a scripture reading, and prayers—which the children joined in whispers—Ann stopped worrying they would act up like her past students and began to worry they might never speak around her at all. Next, she passed around slates and pencils so the children could copy out Psalm 23. *The Lord is my shepherd,* Ann thought, bracing herself as she wrote the words out for her students to copy. Surely if a commotion were going to start, it would be now. But all she heard, just before instruction began, was a single soft "Baaa . . . baaa. . ."

Judging by his sheepish smile when she turned around, Ann suspected the culprit was a child she recognized from King's Arms Tavern. She opened her mouth to scold the boy, but paused when a fit of stifled giggles rippled through the tense, silent classroom. Faced with thirty pairs of nervous eyes awaiting her reaction, Ann merely gave the class a rather stern look and began the lesson. Within minutes, the room was full of the scratching of slate pencils as her students focused on forming their letters. Ann breathed a sigh of relief. At the end of the day, she taught her students one last thing, and a chorus of smiling children recited Benjamin Franklin's words with her: "Tis easier to prevent bad habits than to break them."

In 1763, just three years after the Bray School opened, Benjamin Franklin himself returned to Williamsburg because his good friend, Mr. Hunter, had died. No doubt by this time the Bray School was very successful. Though records don't tell us for sure, certainly Mr. Franklin would want to check on the school's progress with Robert Carter Nicholas, who had taken charge of the institution after Reverend Dawson died. If Benjamin Franklin did visit her school, Ann must surely have been delighted and a bit nervous. Can you imagine giving Benjamin Franklin a tour of your school?

For almost ten whole years, educated, well-mannered children graduated from Ann Wager's amazing school. All was going well, until the afternoon a gloomy Robert Carter Nicholas stopped by.

"Mrs. Wager, I am sorry to say we have very little money," he told her. "We have no choice. We must close the Bray School."

This news was worse than being caught outside in a thunderstorm. "Surely there must be a way to continue. These students are doing so well," Ann said.

Robert Carter Nicholas shook his head. "Taxes are increasing. Things are changing, Mrs. Wager. Money to support the school has stopped coming from England."

Ann looked around the room. She thought about the children. She heard their voices in her memory, reciting Psalm 23. "My needs are few. I can live on little or no salary," she said.

Robert Carter Nicholas accepted Ann's offer to allow her to work for very little money. Now it was possible for the school to stay open—and stay open it did, for five more years! The Bray School only closed when Ann, the beloved teacher who had made a difference in the lives of so many children, died in 1774.

Old school records are not always accurate. However, there is evidence to suggest that Gowan Pamphlet, an enslaved man who eventually gained his freedom and was greatly respected as the first African American Baptist minister in Williamsburg, could have been a student of hers. In fact, some people believe that Gowan Pamphlet was one of the children who came to the Bray School from the King's Arms Tavern. Do you suppose that sometimes when he preached, he thought about Ann Wager, Psalm 23, and Noah's Ark?

What was Ann Wager's revolutionary WOW factor? Why do you think she was so eager to accept this challenge? Was it her compassion for the children? Was it her generosity? Was it her love of education? In what ways do you think Ann helped her students become the best they could be?

Elizabeth Freeman
1742-1829

At the end of the Eighteenth Century, Boston, another city under British control, was a bustling Massachusetts seaport. Merchants placed orders in their shops, then sold the products that arrived on ships from England. Then, without warning, high taxes were placed on paint, glass, lamp oil, and other products imported by the British. The merchants began to lose customers because people refused to buy the taxed British goods.

The last straw was the tax on tea. In 1773, the colonists took action. Dressed as Native Americans, they climbed aboard three ships belonging to Britain's powerful East India Company and dumped all the chests of tea on board into Boston Harbor. This was called the Boston Tea Party. But even more drastic changes were coming. Sometime in 1775, the British announced that the colony of Massachusetts was in a state of rebellion. Local leaders even wrote a new constitution for Massachusetts. The new state constitution was adopted in 1780.

During this time, there lived an observant enslaved woman with no formal education, who listened quietly during many meetings between important men in the home she was bound to. These gatherings led to big changes in the constitution of Massachusetts. One change was the abolition of slavery in that state. Is it possible that, as a result of her observations, she might someday come to be known as one of the wisest women in the state? That is for you to decide after you learn more about Elizabeth Freeman. Her story, like so many others, has been pieced together from letters, journals, and stories that have been shared through generations. While we cannot know everything about her life, there are certain facts that many sources agree upon.

THE PATIENT LISTENER

Way back in 1742, long before the Revolutionary War, the woman who would one day be called Elizabeth Freeman was born to enslaved parents, property of a Dutch family who lived in New York state. Back then, she was just Elizabeth, and she was called Bett. She had a little sister named Lizzie. When they were teenagers, Bett and Lizzie were given as a wedding gift to Hannah, the Dutchman's bad-tempered daughter. After Hannah married John Ashley, they moved to Sheffield, Massachusetts.

John Ashley was a wealthy lawyer. His home was a popular meeting place for many important people in town. Since the gentlemen were concerned about increased British control in the American colonies, these meetings sometimes lasted for hours. People wanted to enjoy their lives and not be bothered by British rule. Often, a young lawyer named Theodore Sedgewick led them in discussions about the importance of individual rights.

During these discussions about the new laws and taxes being heaped on the people of the colonies, Bett was always in the room, serving bread and cheeses and cold meats. She kept hot tea in the teapot. And all the while, Bett listened quietly while the men talked politics.

What Bett didn't realize was that she was overhearing ideas that would be included in a constitution for the new Commonwealth of Massachusetts. But she probably gave considerable thought to one particular discussion: a discussion of the idea that all people were born free and equal. *Why certainly,* she must have thought, *if all are born free and created equal, then I believe I should be included too.* Thoughts of living life as a free person must have swirled in her head as Bett went about her daily duties.

Then, one horrible day, Bett heard an angry commotion in the kitchen. Miss Hannah was never pleased about anything. Today, her screaming rage was directed right at Bett's sister, Lizzie.

"This chicken is stringy and dry. Why don't you learn to roast a chicken! Look at these beans! Nothing but mush!" Miss Hannah flung a huge spoonful of steaming beans at Lizzie. "And these biscuits!" Hannah threw the basket of biscuits on the floor and stomped on one. "You made these biscuits hard on purpose. You want me to break a tooth!"

Bett could hardly believe her eyes. In the corner near the fireplace, Lizzie crouched low, covering her face with her hands to protect herself. Then, Miss Hannah pulled a small coal shovel from the hearth, still red-hot from the blazing fire, and rushed toward Lizzie. In three giant leaps, Bett was across the kitchen and standing between the two. She received a terrible burn on her arm from the red-hot shovel. That ugly scar would remain on her arm forever.

Bett wasted no time. She left the Ashley house as soon as she could and hurried along the road to the nearby town of Stockbridge. There, she searched for the office of the attorney Theodore Sedgwick. At the Ashley house, she had heard him discuss freedom and equality for all. She hoped maybe, just maybe, he could help her. At last, she found his office. Bett pounded on the door until, much to her relief, Mr. Sedgwick opened it.

"Well, hello, Bett. Come in, come in," he said. "What brings you here?" Mr. Sedgwick seemed surprised and happy to see her. He welcomed her into his office. Bett removed her woolen cloak and rolled up her sleeve. Mr. Sedgwick's smile faded to anger as he examined the burn. Bett told him of her difficult life in the Ashley household. When Mr. Sedgwick replied, she knew she had placed her trust in the right person. "Bett, we are going to court. It may take some time, but I believe there is a way to end this. You will live as a free woman and not as a slave."

"Oh, Mr. Sedgwick, I will be so grateful. I don't know how I can ever pay you. . . ."

"Put your worries away, Bett. I have an idea. Will you consider staying with my family? You would be welcome in our home." Bett could hardly believe what she was hearing. Mr. Sedgwick continued, "Our children are little and quite a handful. We have searched for a kind, loving person to help us guide them and care for them. I believe you are just the right person." Bett accepted the offer and moved into the Sedgwick home. There, she began a busy and happy life as the children's nanny.

Mr. Sedgwick was able to join Bett's case with that of a man named Brom, who was also enslaved in the Ashley household and wanted his freedom. The case of Brom and Bett versus J. Ashley Esq. was brought before the court.

During the Revolutionary War, as the colonies battled for independence, Mr. Sedgwick found that he had quite a battle of his own on his hands. John Ashley was determined that Bett would not have her freedom. "She is my property," he insisted again and again to his lawyer, and that is exactly what Ashley's lawyer claimed in court. This difficult problem was easily settled. It turned out that, although Massachusetts had been the first of the American colonies to legalize slavery, thanks to the newly ratified constitution, Massachusetts was also the first colony—now state—to abolish it. All those lively political discussions overheard by Elizabeth now came back to haunt John Ashley.

At last, it was official! In 1781, the court declared

that Bett was not the property of John Ashely. She was a free person. As the first enslaved woman set free under the new Massachusetts constitution, she took the name Elizabeth Freeman.

Bett's life was good. She spent many happy years caring for the Sedgwick children until they were grown, and they loved her like she was family. Catherine, the eldest child, gave her a special nickname: Mumbet. History is fuzzy, but at some point during her years looking after the Sedgwicks, Bett married and had children of her own.

When Bett was choosing "Freeman" as her new last name, she might as well have added "Courage" as her middle name. One blustery winter night, when Mr. Sedgwick was away on business, Mrs. Sedgwick caught a cold and went to bed sick, leaving Bett to care for her as well as the children. Earlier that day, Bett had heard that a gang of robbers was roaming the streets, breaking into houses and frightening the homeowners. They were looking for small, easy-to-carry items—watches, rings, sliver dishes, and other valuables. The robberies were happening near the Sedgwick home. Bett feared the Sedgwicks might be next, so she hid the Sedgwick family silver in her bedroom dresser.

Sure enough, that night, she heard troubling noises. Lifting a candle high so she could see around the house, Bett discovered robbers lurking in the dining room. She suspected they were searching for silver items like serving platters and cream and sugar containers. Bett was silent as she bravely stood watching them. Just as she hoped, the robbers ignored her as they emptied drawers searching for valuables. After all, she was a lowly servant—or so they thought. They did not check her room or look in her dresser. Bett's plan worked. The silver was safe. When the thieves left disappointed, she straightened the house while the children and Mrs. Sedgwick slept.

Even as grownups, the Sedgwick children continued to love their Mumbet. She saved enough of her wages that, when she retired from her job with the Sedgwicks, she could purchase her very own comfortable home. Catherine Sedgwick remained close to her Mumbet as an adult and often visited her. When Bett died on December 28, 1829, a surprising thing happened, perhaps more spectacular than any comet streaking across the sky: Bett was buried in the Sedgwick family cemetery. She is the only person of color—indeed, the only person not related to the Sedgwick family—to be buried there. Her marker is right in the center, very near Catherine. To this day, visitors to the Stockbridge cemetery can read the inscription on her grave marker written by Charles Sedgwick, Catherine's brother:

"Elizabeth Freeman, known by the name of Mumbet died December 28, 1829. Her supposed age was 85 years. She was born a slave and remained a slave for nearly thirty years. She could neither read nor write, yet in her own sphere she had no superior nor equal.

She neither wasted time nor property. She never violated a trust. In every situation of domestic trial, she was the most efficient helper, and the tenderest friend. Good mother, fare well."

What do you think was Elizabeth Freeman's revolutionary WOW factor? When did she develop her strong sense of what was right and what was wrong? Why did being a good listener help her? How do you know she was courageous?

Nancy Morgan Hart
1753-1830

In 1733, Georgia, named for King George II, was the last colony to be recognized as one of the original Thirteen Colonies. The first Englishman to settle in the region was James Oglethorpe. He encouraged folks who were looking for a fresh beginning after being released from debtors' prison to settle in Georgia. Some became farmers, raising rice, indigo, and other crops for export. Savannah, the capital of Georgia, became a busy seaport. Unlike the residents of many other seaport cities in the American colonies, the citizens there felt safe and happy under

British control because they knew the British would protect their seaport from invasion by Spanish ships in the area, as well as from attacks by local Native Americans. People who supported the British at this time were known as Tories. However, the people who lived away from the coast were independent and self-sufficient. They were also Loyalists—people in favor of independence from the British Crown. They did not support the British when the Revolutionary War eventually reached Georgia.

A TURKEY TALE

Living out in the wilderness of North Georgia's mountains in the late 1700s was not easy, but Nancy Morgan Hart was up to the task. After many seasons of hoeing corn rows, tending her herb garden, and chopping wood, she had the strength of any man. At some point, she earned the respect of the Cherokee Indians who were her neighbors. According to some legends, they even gave her the nickname "War Woman." Was this because of her fierce blue eyes and fiery red hair? Or perhaps because of her patience and self-confidence? It is difficult to know for certain, because very little has been written about Nancy. Most of the stories we do have were passed down through many generations.

But one tale that stands out might just give us our answer. It's the story of the day Nancy had to dig deep within herself to confront a problem. She had to draw on all her patience and self-confidence to protect her family from six British soldiers.

Nancy was almost always patient with her children.

She kept them so busy with chores that they didn't have time to get into much mischief. She also tried to be patient when she caught deer munching on her corn. She understood that deer got hungry, and she knew they didn't mean any harm.

But British soldiers got hungry too. A group of six British soldiers often stopped by to take Nancy's food. They constantly snooped around, suspecting she might be a spy for the Loyalist cause. Nancy tried to be patient with these rude and bossy soldiers as well. But there came a day when the British soldiers got on her last nerve.

It started when one of her children, who had been pulling weeds in the garden, burst into the cabin. "Ma! Ma! The British soldiers are back—and all six are chasing Tom!"

Nancy was furious. Tom was the last male turkey in their flock. She dropped her mending and ran from the cabin, red hair flying. She yelled in the loudest voice possible, "Get away from my turkey!"

But it was too late. *Boom!* went a musket, and feathers flew everywhere. One of the soldiers had shot Tom Turkey.

The officer in charge shoved the turkey, feathers and all, right into Nancy's arms. "Cook this!" he ordered.

While she plucked the feathers from dear Tom Turkey, Nancy summoned her patience and gathered her thoughts. She was confident now. She secretly smiled as she cooked up a plan. *I will fix a feast with an unfortunate ending for the British soldiers. Sad as I am that Tom is gone, that good old turkey deserves a proper roasting.* Nancy rubbed the turkey's skin with bear fat and salt. She stuffed him with wild sage from her garden, then hung him on the spit in the fireplace to cook just the right height above the fire. Taking her own sweet time, she then set about gathering the ingredients to make corn cakes drizzled with wild honey.

The six hungry soldiers soon grew impatient for their meal. They pushed their way into the cabin. One at a time, they stacked their muskets against the wall near the door and sat wherever they could find space on the cabin floor. Seeing their scowling faces, Nancy held up a small jug. "Care for some blackberry juice?" she asked.

"No," said the officer in charge. "We want that jug." He pointed his skinny finger at a big pottery jug that belonged to Nancy's husband. It was full to the top with homemade corn whiskey.

Careful not to spill it, Nancy used both hands to carry the jug across the room to the soldiers. While she mixed the batter for the corn cakes, she watched from the corner of her eye. The greedy soldiers gulped again and again from the jug. *I must be patient,* she thought. *Soon enough, the soldiers will get sleepy from too much drink.* She was right. At last, the soldiers drifted, snoring, into sleep. Nancy whispered to one of her children, "Don't say a word. Go outside and wait by the little window. I am going to pass the muskets out to you. Your job is to hide them."

One, two, three, four, five—Nancy unloaded the muskets and passed them through the window to the child waiting outside. Musket number six, Nancy placed at her side. While she and the children feasted on turkey and corn cakes drizzled with wild honey, the six British soldiers continued to snore.

It is believed that Nancy held the British soldiers prisoner until her husband returned home. What happened after that is history's secret. But in 1912, plans were underway to grade the land to lay railroad tracks near where Nancy's cabin once stood. What do you think the workmen found under several feet of earth? Six skeletons buried in a row.

In 1933, the Daughters of the American Revolution reconstructed Nancy Morgan Hart's cabin. Stones from the original chimney were used to build the chimney in the new cabin. Wouldn't it be amazing if those stones could tell us about one special turkey dinner?

An organization called Georgia Women of Achievement researches and offers educational materials about the amazing women in Georgia's history. In 1996, this organization recognized Nancy Morgan Hart as one such amazing woman.

What do you think was Nancy Morgan Hart's revolutionary WOW factor? How loyal was she to her country? When did she have to use patience? In what ways was she self-confident under pressure?

Polly Cooper
17??-18??

A spirit of change was coming. Wanting to be free from British rule, the colonies were in revolt. Representatives from each of the Thirteen Colonies had signed the Declaration of Independence in 1776, and the Revolutionary War was now underway.

General George Washington knew that our new United States would need a flag. In 1776, he approved a flag designed with thirteen red and white alternating stripes. Thirteen stars representing the Thirteen Colonies were added in 1777. General Washington also oversaw the training of the American troops. He knew the troops had to be prepared for big battles and little skirmishes alike. But what General Washington did not foresee was the terrible winter of 1777, when his troops would be in danger, not from musket fire on the battlefield, but from starvation in their own camp at Valley Forge.

FRIENDS FOREVER

Would you walk more than four hundred miles—through snow drifts nearly as tall as you are, in below-freezing temperatures—to bring food to a friend? In the winter of 1777, Polly Cooper, along with forty or so other members of the Oneida Indian Nation, did just that. Through the worst possible conditions, they carried bushels of white corn to George Washington's starving troops at Valley Forge, Pennsylvania, that dreadful winter.

The relationship between the Oneida people and American troops was cemented during the Battle of Saratoga in New York, just months before the difficult winter of 1777. Some of the Oneidas had acted as scouts, reporting British troop movements. Others fought side by side with the Continental Army. It was a tough battle, but with the help of the Oneidas, the Continental Army prevented the British from marching up the Mohawk River Valley to capture Albany, New York. This victory created a lasting friendship between the Oneida Chief Skenandoah, his warriors, and George Washington's troops. In fact, the Oneidas were the first sovereign nation to acknowledge the United States as a country.

Winter came early in 1777. The weather was brutally cold, but the Oneidas were tucked safely in their warm homes. Their storehouses were filled with white corn. They were prepared for a harsh winter. Then, word came to the Oneida settlement that their friends, the American soldiers, were in a very bad way at their camp in Valley Forge, just outside of Philadelphia, Pennsylvania. The brave soldiers were dressed only in raggedy uniforms, and many did not have shoes. They were starving and suffering terribly from various sicknesses. No matter how General Washington pleaded for funds to help his troops, no help came.

When Polly Cooper, a young Oneida maiden, heard of the dreadful situation, she went to Chief Skenandoah with an unusual idea. "I heard our brave soldier friends are suffering from the winter weather. They could be starving. Once again, we must help them. Chief Skenandoah, if you organize a group to bring white corn to General Washington and his troops, I will go along to make sure they know how to cook it."

"It is winter, and the snow is deep. I will ask and see what happens," the chief said. Forty-one Oneida Indians, including Polly, were willing to hike over four hundred miles to Valley Forge. The plan was to take as much white corn as they could carry to their starving friends, show them how to prepare it, and then come home.

The journey was long, and the weather was bad, but Polly and the others were prepared. Eventually, they reached Valley Forge. Polly's heart sank. She could hardly believe her eyes. *What has happened? Everywhere I look, I see starving, raggedy soldiers. They once stood so tall and proud.* A few desperate soldiers tried to grab the white corn from the sacks and gnaw it right off the cob.

"Stop right now," Polly said. "This is not yellow corn. It is white corn. You can't eat it uncooked." Polly knew the dangers of eating raw white corn. "Your stomachs can't tolerate it. You will be sicker than you are now." It soon became clear to Polly that it was up to her to step up and take charge. Polly said to her traveling companions, "Please find a big kettle, a jug of water, and a stack of firewood." Her Oneida companions helped her set up a little outside kitchen. Polly boiled some corn until it was soft. Then, she cut the corn from the cob using a sharp hunting knife and mixed the corn with more water in the kettle to make a smooth, creamy soup. "This is just what these soldiers need," she said to her companions. Polly moved through the camp, and as she spooned the soup into the open mouths of any soldiers too weak to feed themselves, she smiled and thought of a mother bird feeding her babies.

Day after day, Polly fixed more corn. She pounded dried corn into meal. From this, she made a nourishing hot cereal. Eventually, when the men could eat solid food, she mashed some of the cooked white corn, mixed it with flour, and shaped corn cakes. She cooked these cakes in big black skillets. Polly had planned well before leaving home. She used dried plants she had brought with her to make a nourishing tea for the men. Gradually, the soldiers got stronger.

Finally, the time came for the Oneidas to make the four-hundred-mile trip back to their village, but Polly felt the deep commitment of friendship toward the soldiers. "Please go on without me. When I see that it is time for me to leave here, I will find my way home," she said to her traveling companions. "I must stay at Valley Forge. These soldiers need someone to take care of them until they are strong again."

She gave generously of her time to teach the soldiers and the wives who accompanied them about tasty ways to cook and serve white corn. Most of the women stayed in local houses and came to the camp during the day to take care of the soldiers. One woman who was especially grateful to Polly Cooper was Martha Washington, the wife of General George Washington. Martha and George were staying in the comfort of a warm house not far from the camp.

Eventually, the soldiers were strong enough to resume their duties. Polly said to her friends, "Now, it is time for me to return to my people."

The folks had grown to love Polly. "Oh Polly," one of the grateful wives said, "we are sorry you have to leave, but we understand. We have taken up a collection to pay you for your help."

Polly was generous by nature. "I can't accept money. This was something my heart called on me to do."

When Polly refused pay for looking after the soldiers, the women met with Martha Washington. They tried to think of the best way to thank Polly for her friendship and generosity. They surprised Polly with a gift: a beautiful black lace shawl. She said, "I shall treasure this shawl and the memories that come with it." Polly took special care of the shawl, as did her descendants. It has been preserved and passed down through many generations of her family.

Today, the Oneida Indian Nation considers the beautiful black shawl a symbol of the lasting friendship between the Oneida people and the Americans. Occasionally, it is put on display. In 2005, the Oneida County Historical Society officially recognized Polly Cooper for her contribution to the American Revolution. She is now a member of the Oneida County Historical Society Hall of Fame, along with Oneida Chief Skenandoah, who was recognized in 2002. If you visit the Smithsonian Museum of the American Indian in Washington, DC, you will see a statue honoring Polly Cooper.

What do you think was Polly Cooper's revolutionary WOW factor? How did she show generosity? When did she show compassion? In what ways could you show you care about a friend?

Betty Zane
1765-1823

In 1716, Alexander Spottswood, the British Royal Governor of Virginia, had an interesting idea. He planned a trip into the western part of Virginia to claim more land for King George I. Some believe he was also looking for natural resources, such as coal or lumber. It was a rugged trip for Governor Spottswood and his companions. Because this was land unexplored by the people of the colonies, the party had to cross many streams and chop their way through underbrush and brambles. Fortunately, the travelers brought extra horseshoes because the trip was difficult on their horses' hooves. Some of the travelers' fine clothing was damaged beyond repair. When they came upon the beautiful Shenandoah Valley, nestled in the shadow of the Blue Ridge Mountains, they decided it was time to head home.

After they returned to Williamsburg, news spread quickly about the newly explored land. Before long, people had loaded up wagons and headed toward the mountains. To people with a rugged pioneering spirit, the other side of the mountains must have sounded like a perfect place. Although some settled in the Shenandoah Valley, others crossed the mountains. But eventually, serious struggles began between the travelers and the Native Americans, who had signed a treaty with the British that made it illegal for colonists to settle in the land beyond the Blue Ridge Mountains.

When the Revolutionary War ended and the British treaty was overturned, those struggles would only intensify. . . .

THE AMAZING RUN

Do you know what it means to be courageous? It means you don't let being afraid stop you from doing the things you need to do. Do you know a courageous person? If so, you may be reminded of them when you meet Betty Zane, a courageous teenage girl who loved her brothers very much. As you read her story, you will see just how courageous she was.

Betty Zane and her five adventurous older brothers grew up in Virginia along the Potomac River. Rarely did a girl living in these times leave home to get schooling, but dark-haired, dark-eyed Betty did. When Betty was a teenager, her parents sent her to Philadelphia to live with relatives. There, she attended school and learned social graces. But while people were struggling against British rule, the spirit of revolution grew in cities and towns, including Philadelphia, and high-spirited Betty conducted a revolution of her own. She was tired of wearing fancy dresses and toe-pinching shoes.

This daring and adventurous teenager left Philadelphia with a plan to travel over the mountains in search of her two most favorite brothers, Ebenezer and Silas. No e-mail. No cell phones. No texting. Yet somehow, she received information that her brothers had traveled far beyond the Shenandoah Valley into the wilderness of western Virginia, to a place that is now called Wheeling, West Virginia.

She did not want to be left behind. *Crazy brothers.... Who mends their britches, makes the biscuits, and roasts potatoes for them out there in the wilderness?* She laughed at the thought of her brothers looking after themselves. *I don't want to be apart from Ebenezer and Silas for one more minute. I miss them too much. I don't care how far I have to travel into the wilderness, I will find them.*

That is exactly what Betty did. How she got there and with whom she traveled is a mystery. Did she ride horseback? Could she have walked? Perhaps. But most likely, she traveled by supply wagon, snuggled down between bags of flour and cornmeal so as not bounce around too much.

Traveling into the wilderness was dangerous. There were no interstates or fast-food restaurants. The roads were little more than poorly marked trails. Along the way, supply wagons would stop at forts to make deliveries. Betty learned that, for safety, pioneering people built their log homes as near the forts as they could. There was plenty of conflict between the pioneers and the Native Americans who lived west of the mountains, because a treaty signed many years before made it illegal for pioneers to settle beyond the Appalachians. But this treaty had been signed by the British government. Although the Revolutionary War hadn't yet ended, many people in the American colonies decided to cross the mountains anyway. As for Betty, she merely wanted to find her brothers.

Each morning, Betty closed her eyes, crossed her fingers, and made this wish: *I wish, I wish tonight is a night we stay at a fort. I am hungry for a bowl of good stew instead of hard biscuits and chewy dried meat by a campfire.* She also appreciated sleeping on a bed instead of the hard ground. Camping on the trail was so creepy. During those nights she slept on the ground, Betty wrapped her cloak tightly around her and huddled close to the campfire. She knew it was dangerous beyond the firelight. Sometimes, her thoughts went wild. There could be Native war bands in the darkness, or hungry bears and poisonous snakes.

After many long days on the trail, Betty heard the wagon driver call out, "Final destination ahead!" As soon as the driver stopped the horses, Betty gathered her skirt and jumped from the wagon. She stood in a clearing that overlooked a small group of cabins nestled in a river valley. The driver called to her, "That's the Ohio River."

Curls of smoke drifted up from some of the cabin chimneys. At the far end of the valley stood a fort atop a small hill, surrounded by a tall fence. *This is the place!*

My brothers are here, and here is where I want to be. She stood in the afternoon sunshine, took a deep breath, and stretched her arms up to the blue sky. "This place is so much better than a crowded city," she said aloud.

Not waiting for the wagon, Betty galloped at full speed down the hill toward the cluster of cabins. As she approached the cabins, she cupped her hands around her mouth and called, "Ebenezer! Silas! Ebenezer! Silas!" A woman bouncing a baby on her hip waved her apron to get Betty's attention and pointed to a cabin less than a hundred yards from the fort. Betty's heart nearly pounded out of her chest. At the far side of the cabin, a familiar figure was bent low, digging in a garden. Hearing her voice, he stood up, shading his eyes from the sun. It was her beloved Ebenezer. Betty ran to him faster than any deer through the forest. Taking a flying leap into his outstretched arms, she brought them both tumbling to the ground in a laughing heap. When Ebenezer told her Silas lived at the fort, she took off running at top speed to find him as well.

The fort in the clearing was called Fort Henry, after the Virginian patriot Patrick Henry. Betty arrived at the settlement sometime in the spring before Lord Cornwallis and his British troops surrendered in Yorktown, Virginia, on October 19, 1781, ending the Revolutionary War. But news of the surrender was slow to reach the British troops in the wilderness. So, off and on for the next year, British soldiers continued to attack Fort Henry, believing they were still at war.

Warriors from the Delaware and Wyandot Tribes often traveled with the British. These Tribes, fighting to reclaim their land, shared the British goal: to destroy the pioneering people. The soldiers had firearms, and the Native warriors used bows and arrows, some with poison tips, as well as sharp tomahawks to scalp pioneering people.

With so many enemies lurking around, none of the pioneering people felt completely safe. Nevertheless, the women planted corn and beans, or cabbage and potatoes. They tended their gardens and gathered nuts and wild berries. The men hunted deer, rabbits, and squirrels. Sometimes, they ate fish snared from the nearby Ohio River. The pioneering people may have brought a cow or two, some sheep, or chickens with them, so they had milk and eggs. Some women brought spinning wheels. They built looms so the women could weave woolen yarn into fabric to make clothes. Although life wasn't easy, Betty was happy to finally be with her brothers.

She quickly learned that when she and the others heard the words, "To fort! To fort!" not to question or waste a minute. Danger was nearby. They had to stop right in the middle of what they were doing and run lickety-split to Fort Henry. Inside, there was shelter for thirty or so families. When the last family was safely inside, the heavy gates were closed and locked, and the people within waited and waited . . . sometimes for days.

Despite the hardships, sixteen-year-old Betty adjusted quickly to pioneering life. No more brocade dresses and pinching shoes. Her apron became her best friend. Betty could gather eggs into her apron and carry them unbroken to the cabin. She used her apron to wipe perspiration from her face. When she took freshly made biscuits to Silas at the fort, she piled the hot biscuits in her apron, gathered the sides together, and sprinted up the hill. Because she could run so fast, the biscuits were always still hot when she gave them to Silas.

Life continued in this way for some time, until one September day in 1782, nearly a year after the British had surrendered at Yorktown. The leaves were golden and flame-colored. Autumn's first chill was in the air. Ebenezer split firewood for winter. Betty dug up the last of the potatoes.

"Is there any truth to what the women are saying?" Betty called to Ebenezer from the garden.

"What did those cackling hen women say now?"

"They say that the British and Indians—possibly Delaware and Wyandots—may be circling around to get us again!"

"It's usually just the Wyandots," said Ebenezer.

"When I left Philadelphia, I didn't want to see another British Red Coat."

"I'll head on up to the fort. Maybe they have a new scouting report."

Betty put her hands on her hips, and her dark eyes

shot fire at him. "Ebenezer Zane! Don't you dare volunteer to go wilderness scouting."

A clanging bell at the fort stopped their conversation. The dreaded words "To fort! To fort!" spread from cabin to cabin. Everybody raced to the fort. Mothers carried infants on their hips and dragged little children by the hand. Betty ran at full speed, still clutching her apron full of potatoes.

At last, all the pioneering people were safely inside the fort. The heavy gate was closed and secured. There was no time to waste. Preparations to defend Fort Henry began. Everyone had tasks. Some women cooked and some looked after the smaller children. Others tore cloth to make bandages.

Betty had already proved that she was as brave as her brothers. In past attacks, she had handled difficult tasks. Today, her job was melting lead in a giant ladle over a hot fire. With a steady hand, she poured the liquid lead into musket ball molds. Her work didn't end there. Slowly and carefully so she didn't burn herself, she placed the hot molds in a bucket of water to cool them. Then she began again, melting lead for another batch of musket balls.

During the night, a scout returned to Fort Henry with troubling news. British soldiers, along with Native warriors in war dress, were close enough to attack. The commander of the fort sent a messenger to another fort to ask for reinforcements. But before help could come, Fort Henry came under attack. Betty worked for forty hours making musket balls. She was hot and tired, but she did not stop until she heard terrible news.

"We are almost out of black powder," the commander of Fort Henry said. "Without black powder, we can't fire our muskets. If help doesn't come soon, we are in real danger."

Betty heard Ebenezer's voice through the whooping and gunfire. "I have a keg of black powder hidden in my cabin. I'll go get it."

"Nonsense," said the commander. "I can't afford to lose another man. I'll send one of the younger boys."

Betty knew exactly where the black powder was hidden. "Let me go," she said. "They won't fire at a girl." Without waiting for a yes or no, Betty hugged Ebenezer, and he opened the gate just wide enough to for her to slip through. Betty took off running through the clearing. The distance to the cabin was almost the length of a football field. She heard shouting, but no musket fire. She didn't have to dodge arrows. Inside the cabin, the light was dim, but that didn't matter. Betty pushed a heavy trunk aside and moved a basket of blankets. There, tucked in its hiding place, was the keg of black powder! Slowly, carefully, she rolled the keg to the center of the room. *Now what should I do? The keg is too heavy to carry!* Time was precious. Betty stayed calm. *I know exactly what I will do.* She opened the keg and emptied as much black powder into her apron as it would hold. Then she tied the corners of her apron together so the black powder would not spill. She took a deep breath. *I know I can do this. I will run fast, faster than when I carry hot biscuits to the fort for Silas.*

Slowly, she opened the cabin door and looked around. No one was in the clearing. But she knew the enemies were watching from their hiding places in the woods. "I can do this, I can do this, I can do this," she whispered, then took off running. Her feet hardly touched the ground. Now the British and the Native warriors saw her running with something in her apron. They knew it was time to stop the runner. The British fired their muskets. Arrows whistled past Betty's head, and her heart beat faster and faster. *I can do this. I can make the last few yards.* The gate swung open, and there were Ebenezer and Silas. No time for hugs. Betty carefully handed them the bundled apron. The black powder meant the guns could fire again.

It was two days before help arrived from Fort Pitt. Because of Betty Zane's amazing run, Fort Henry was able to hold off the attackers until then. This came to be known as the final battle of the Revolutionary War.

Peace finally came to the Ohio Valley soon after. Betty Zane married and raised a family right across the river, in a place now called Martins Ferry, Ohio. She is buried near her beloved brother, Ebenezer, at Walnut Grove Cemetery in Martins Ferry. Over time, the children of the community raised money for a statue of Betty Zane. This statue stands at the entrance to the cemetery. Many years later, Zane Gray, one of Betty's descendants, became a writer. He wrote of his great-great aunt's adventures as a pioneering person.

Betty Zane risked her life in a daring run carrying black powder. If she had been hit by a musket ball, the powder would have blown up and taken her with it. What do you think was Betty Zane's revolutionary WOW factor? Was she brave or reckless? How do you know she loved her family? Why do you think she had a sense of responsibility to her wilderness community?

Dolley Madison
1768-1849

America, a young and independent nation, continued to grow in many ways. The capital was moved from
Philadelphia to the newly established city of Washington, DC. John Adams, the second president of the
United States, signed an act in 1800 establishing the
Library of Congress. He moved the expanding library,
which included books from the personal libraries of
important Virginians such as Thomas Jefferson and
Peyton Randolph, to Washington, DC, from Philadelphia. No one suspected that by 1812, this growing nation would be embroiled in another war with England.

It began on the Atlantic Ocean, when the British navy tried to interrupt American trade with other countries. British war ships stopped American merchant ships, captured American sailors, and forced them to serve on British ships. Eventually, British troops invaded the new nation, and America was once again at war.

THE HEROINE HOSTESS

Would you lean out the window of the White House in Washington, DC, with a spy glass, looking for danger? Do you think the wife of the president of the United States would be that daring? If you said yes, you are correct. Dolley Madison, the wife of James Madison, the fourth president of the United States, did exactly that.

Dolley's road to the White House began a long way from Washington, DC. Born in Guilford County, North Carolina, she eventually married and moved to Philadelphia. Philadelphia was the center of political activity in the new United States, where important decisions were made and spectacular parties were thrown by wealthy men and their wives. Dolley enjoyed an exciting life in the city. After her first husband died, she married James Madison. Now, her real adventure was about to begin. For a while, the Madisons lived in Virginia. James busied himself with politics, and Dolley soon gained a reputation as a hostess who hosted elegant parties.

Shortly after their close friend, Thomas Jefferson, was elected the third president of the United States, he asked James Madison to be his secretary of state. James accepted. Dolley was thrilled. They began making preparations to move to the bustling city of Washington, DC. "Where will we live in Washington?" she asked James. "Have you sent someone ahead to locate a house for us?"

"Dearest wife," James said, "how would you like to live in the president's house?"

"Live in the president's house?" Dolley could not believe her good fortune.

"President Jefferson's wife died a long time ago. He has no one to plan his social events. If we live there, he will call upon you to plan parties and arrange formal entertaining."

"Oh yes! Oh yes! I will plan the best parties for our president."

After meeting with President Jefferson and officially accepting his offer, Dolley was nearly speechless—but not quite. "I will be delighted to oversee the social activities. It is an honor to serve you, Mr. President, and our country," she said. "I have just one request, Mr. President. Would you please make your ice cream recipe available to me?"

Thomas Jefferson fulfilled Dolley's request. He'd acquired quite a taste for ice cream while he was in France during the Revolutionary War. It is reported that he enjoyed ice cream so much that he brought recipes home with him. He also brought a special machine with detailed directions for making the tasty frozen treat. To Thomas Jefferson's delight, Dolley served plenty of ice cream during the time she served as his hostess.

Eventually, the Madisons moved into their own home . . . but not for long. After Thomas Jefferson's term as president ended, James Madison was elected the fourth president of the United States, and Dolley was back in the White House. Her social and event planning skills once again shone. Dolley organized the first ever Inaugural Ball held in the White House, and from there she continued to dazzle everyone, from foreign dignitaries to her husband's political opponents, with impressive parties and lavish dinners.

Four years passed in the blink of an eye. James was such a popular president that he was re-elected for a second term, and Dolley was planning another Inaugural Ball! Do you know what that meant? As First Lady, Dolley happily served ice cream to her guests for eight years. As a matter of fact, historians tell us she loved ice cream so much that she made it the official dessert of state dinners. Although President Jefferson's favorite recipe used only frozen cream, sugar, and fruit, Dolley experimented with other flavors. Pretend that Dolley Madison has invited you to a fancy dinner. You are not served strawberry or blackberry ice cream. What do you see in your fancy bowl? It could be asparagus or oyster or parmesan cheese ice cream. Using your best manners, what would you do? What would you say?

Life as the First Lady wasn't all about parties, though. As First Lady, Dolley loved and respected the flag, the government, and most of all, the American people. She had also grown up with seven brothers and sisters in a warm home, with plenty of food and loving parents. So her heart must have broken when she learned about the many homeless orphaned children, especially little girls, living on the streets of Washington, DC. Because she loved all her people, Dolley took action and helped establish a home for orphaned girls.

Then, the worst possible thing happened! British troops returned to invade the new United States of America. This was called the War of 1812. The real test of Dolley's service to her country was yet to come. And come it did, on a dreadful August morning in 1814.

James gave a great sigh as he sat down at the breakfast table. He placed a folded paper beside his plate. "Dolley my dear, the news is not good."

Something was terribly wrong. Dolley's heart flip-flopped in her chest. "What has happened to upset you like this?"

"The British are coming closer to Washington. I must leave to go meet with my generals. I fear very soon this town will fall under British control."

Dolley put down her teacup. "The British just won't give up, will they? We won our independence.

There was a treaty signed, and now here they come again!"

"I hope to return before the British invade the city," James said. "But I must ask this favor: If I don't get back in time, do you think you could load a wagon with our possessions, a few important documents, and quickly leave town?" He handed her a folded piece of paper. "Directions to a place where we can meet are on this paper."

It is easy to believe that Dolley took her husband's hands in hers in that moment and looked James directly in the eyes. "You know I am strong. I love you, and I love our country. I will do whatever is required of me."

As it turned out, Dolley Madison was as skilled at planning an evacuation as she was at planning a party. She passed out spyglasses to the small group of staff who remained with her. "We will keep a lookout for the British from every window. If we need to go to the rooftop, we will."

So, she and the staff waited and waited. To pass the time, Dolley wrote a letter to her sister describing events as they unfolded. Peeking out the window, she could see people leaving the city. From the roof she could see an even greater distance. One evening, knowing the British were very close, she went up to the roof to have a look around. The way out of the city appeared clear. Then, as she looked through her spyglass, she saw in the distance British troops marching directly toward Washington, DC.

Having no intention of being taken prisoner, Dolley gave the order to evacuate. But she didn't follow James's instructions to load only their personal possessions and papers into a carriage. In fact, she left most of their personal possessions behind. Instead, she filled the wagon with important books, historical documents, and papers. "I know I am forgetting something. What is it?" She took one last look around. "George Washington!" She stopped in front of a huge portrait of George Washington that hung on a wall. She tugged and pulled and pushed this way and that, but the portrait would not budge. She must have been thinking, *Come on, George! Help me out here. I am not leaving without you, for goodness's sake! You defeated the British. They surrendered to you at Yorktown. I am not going to let them take you prisoner now!*

Someone shouted from outside, "Hurry, Mrs. Madison! The wagon is loaded, and the British are advancing."

"I am not leaving the White House without George Washington!"

But it was no use. The frame was bolted to the wall. Finally, Dolley called out for help. She and the staff pounded and pounded at the heavy frame until it broke in several spots. Carefully, Dolley removed the painting, rolled up the canvas, then hustled to the wagon.

The British did come to town. They took over the president's house, ate his food, stole what they could carry, then set the place on fire. The damage was terrible, but the war ended not long after. For the remainder of James's second term, he and Dolley lived in another residence in Washington. To keep everyone's spirits up, Dolley probably continued to serve ice cream. Dolley Madison stood by her husband's side through happy times and troublesome times in America. She loved the people and the people loved and admired her until the day she died in her beloved Washington, DC.

Today, the Library of Congress keeps many manuscripts, papers, and books of James Madison's in their collection. One of the major contributors to the Madison Collection was Dolley Madison. Is it possible some of these documents are the very same ones she rescued as she evacuated the White House?

What do you think was Dolley Madison's revolutionary WOW factor? How did she maintain self-confidence under pressure? When did she need the ability to organize? In what ways did she show her patriotic love of country and the American people?

SPECIAL THANKS

A special Thank You goes out to those who contributed to the History of American Women online collection. Their website, listed below, offers biographical information about scores of amazing women who earned their places in American history, from the Colonial period through the Civil War, and provides additional sources for each biography, many of which were of great help in my own research.

Visit their website to find the articles that inspired me to further delve into the stories of the WOW Factor Women in this book!

www.womenhistoryblog.com

ABOUT THE AUTHOR

Heidi Hartwiger is a freelance writer, storyteller, and a writing instructor for Christopher Newport University's LifeLong Learning Program. She has written three nonfiction books, two novels, a children's activity book, and numerous parenting articles. Her writing is archived in the Appalachian Collection at Radford University. Heidi has four adult children and seven grandchildren, who love to visit her at home in Yorktown, Virginia, where she lives with her husband and a shy rescue cat named BooBoo. Her goal is to make the world a better place, one reader at a time.

Visit www.heidihartwiger.com to learn more about Heidi and her work!

Printed in the USA
CPSIA information can be obtained
at www.ICGtesting.com
JSHW021939301223
54587JS00003B/79